Two Emilys

Two Emilys

Poems by

Andrea Potos

Cover design by Shay Culligan
Cover image of Haworth Moor, Yorkshire, UK,
photo by author Andrea Potos
Author photo by Michael Slater

ISBN: 978-1-63980-687-4

Kelsay Books
502 South 1040 East, A-119
American Fork, Utah 84003
Kelsaybooks.com

Acknowledgments

Grateful acknowledgment to the places where some of these poems first appeared:

Calla Press, Loch Raven Review, Poetry East, The Midwest Quarterly, We Lit the Lamps Ourselves (Salmon Poetry, 2012), *Marrow of Summer* (Kelsay Books, 2021), *Her Joy Becomes* (Fernwood Press, 2022), and *Belonging Songs* (Fernwood Press, forthcoming).

And gratitude, again, to Kelsay Books for all they do for poetry.

Contents

For all the women poets

Their books come with me, women writers,
Their verses borne through the rooms
Out between the plum trees to the field,
As an animal will gather things,
A brush, a bone, a shoe,
For comfort against darkness.—

from Gillian Clarke, "Women's Work"

Speaking of Poetry

She said there's a clarity in each word,
like the chandelier
that hung in your dining room as a child—
stars of blue-white and yellow-gold,
even purple and magenta could be found
sparking on all the walls;
each piece of the chandelier—
a teardrop whole and dipped in light—
you could see your whole life through it.

A Stone from Emily Brontë

On the high Yorkshire moor
I found it, dark spotted blue and glazed
with stars and twilight.
One wind-lashed mile away
from her parsonage home,
I bent down to keep it—
dreamed her gaze my own.

Upon Waking

after ED

I'll tell you how the day began—

one dream strand at a time—

pictures sifted in gold-burgundy

the messages, like keys, were lost

Walking the Brontë Moor in Spring

Get your naggy self out there, start
along the public footpath, past the barns
and their newborn lambs curled up in the yards;

begin at the top, alongside tall, bent grasses and gorse,
browned heather and stones and crags—past
Penistone Hill and the reservoir. The wind

is wider up there, let yourself walk
for unmeasured time, the moor air
erase your every last edge.

Brontëan Morning

The loudest crows
cawing over the tops of the oaks
call me to autumn already
and though my back is the window,

I know the sky must be a grey wuthering,
and the curlews are crying. The wind
must be moaning as it goes sweeping
across heath and moors and the spikes
of purple heather thousands of miles away
from where my body sits; yet

I feel the gorse
grazing my ankles as I go.

Three Acorns from Emily's Yard

I pocketed them that day
the tour guide was not looking.

I nodded to myself that she
would not mind for me to hold

in my palm and carry home
such Possibility.

Emily Dickinson Stays Home When Ralph Waldo Emerson Visits Her Brother's House

Let there be no argument
from the grass between
my brother's house and mine.
No need to touch flesh—

like the Word, he must glow.
Hadn't we met in that place
where Dream is born—

I remember—Soul sparks
erupted—I felt
my own ignite—
in my ear—*the Mountains straight reply.*

To Emily Brontë

Eleven years old and sunk in the red velveteen
chair at the Fox Bay Theater, I absorbed
the raw sculpture of Penistone Crag,
bracken and gorse, the peat
blanketing the Yorkshire moors. Heathcliff
with his sea-green eyes, black cape swirled
around him, how tall and alarmingly
handsome he looked.
At Catherine's grave he cried, you wrote:
I cannot live without my life,
desire held hostage in his eyes,

my heart held stunned in my chest.
Years later, I return to your words;
travel to the stone-
flagged floors of your home;
your desk-box saved under glass,
its lining worn, purple velvet
splotched with red sealing wax.
Walking the rocky footpath towards swells
of purple heather, I remember the words
of the local stationer who saw you
returning one evening: *her countenance was lit up*
by a divine light. I imagine
I hear your skin
brush mine, whisper what you know:
the silence, the stars
that burn through the page.
Hone the hours to their core—you might have said—
wind and poem, passion and moor.

To the College Girl Who Sold *The Life of Emily Dickinson*

What can I say to you, twenty years after
you carried the two-volume,
hardcover first edition with illustrations
through the musty portal
of the used bookstore, as if it were
an average day.

Hungry for cash,
you couldn't wait
to unload the books from your pack,
this one gift from your father
when you were a girl of thirteen
dreaming yourself a poet
at your white wooden desk.

How did the years convince you
ten dollars pouring through your fingers—
a bottle of Chianti for that night
and what is long forgotten—surpassed

Awe, the vision
of the woman, the soul at white heat

infinite Circumference of a Life
you'd be craving one day.

To Be Near Emily

A friend who studied at Amherst
told me about the pilgrims who come
leaving scraps of paper, beads and flowers,
hoping to breathe some rarified air.
He and his friends would wait until
the last one wandered off

before they leaned against the stones
in the dusk. They sprawled their legs
on the graveyard grass and rolled joints,
lit them—tiny lasers to pierce the foggy
distance within, as soberly, was her supreme
and daily task.

Brontë Hour

outside the rain-
darkened stones, mist
seeping
through wool
and skin,
inside the fire
speaking sparks,
tossing amber
onto the page
weighted with stories
invisible in air.

A Reading in Emily's House

In the hallway, behind glass,
a white gown stands as welcome.
I tell myself she must be
invisible as music.
Parlor walls lean toward us,
the lamps are lit within as words
unburden themselves to air.
Through the panes, the skies
deepen to amethyst.

Still Life with Emily Brontë

after Nancy Willard

Paint her in what was once the children's study,
sitting, deskbox on her lap.
Let an inkpot rest there,
pen nibs scattered lazily at the top.
Let the shutters be pulled open in eagerness,
her hand be raised
inches off the scarred mahogany surface.
Let the wood anticipate her voice
as she leans into the word,
the moor wind be loud enough
to be a story she hears.

Emily Brontë's Birthday Morning

A full sun strains to burn
through shifting cloud sheaths.
Brightness arrives, then leaves.

I would wring the air with my hands,
haul it over a clothesline to dry if I could.
Nothing minor is occurring.

Somewhere near and unseen,
a mourning dove keeps calling, saying
it is sorrow that keeps the last word.

Portrait of Emily Brontë

Her tall body
like an urn of water

as she flowed from cellar to scullery

out through parsonage doors
to the moor where she met

her match in sky   eyes capturing cloud-race

and blue breaking   travelling
like her hands across paper.

Emily's Door

photograph by Jerome Liebling

From this cut-glass doorknob—
       an angel shot forth

a pistol of light—wings of spears or arrows
as it must be in her Amherst house:

Each doorknob housing
its family of beings

(as floorboards keep their mice
and attic rafters their bats).

Studio Sessions,
Emily Dickinson Museum

This is a mighty room
within its precincts hopes have played.
                                        —E.D.

Two hundred dollars for one hour
may be nothing for the chance
to sit (given one small table and chair)
breathing the air of her room.
Surely some atoms of her being still
linger, though the counterpane
would be new, the lace curtains
pristinely laundered since her touch.

With only pencil and paper (no touching
of the furnishings allowed), how would it be to live
in the aftermath of her? Would she guide
my hand across the modern page?
Could I float along the lost thermals
of her thought? Would ambition keep me
stalled, forgetting how it was
the nobodies she favored.

Emily Dickinson's October Light

That descending
    low-gazing light,

that leaning over light,
    light aslant

like some golden-ochre poem
    borne on the breath of her.

In My Dream of Emily Brontë

She stood in the wind,
handing me the green-
seeped stones
she'd gathered
like aged lichen-
stained words, each
one nestling roughly
beside the other
to make a fence
sprawling across the moor.
Through the spaces
between rock, I knelt
to glimpses of
waterfall, sky,
poems of purple heather.

If Emily Dickinson Made Notes on My Mother's Passing

Oh day of impossibly
blue summer—

the momentous ripening
had come—

her sudden
Intimacy with light—

her blazing clarity
of departure.

Writerly Dream

George Murray Smith, of
Smith, Elder & Co., London, 1847

To have a book accepted
the way the bespectacled editor
leaned back in his creaking, leather chair
one Sunday morning; a manuscript unbound
from twine and brown paper on his lap.
He read and read until the lamps
outside his Cornhill office were lit;
scribbled a hasty note of apology
to the friend he could not meet after all for he
could not stop reading. With only a sandwich
and a glass of wine for sustenance (*the meal,*
a very hasty one, he would later recall), the pages
and pages named *Jane Eyre* held him
long into the London night
and through the centuries to come.

The Last Unread Poems of Charlotte Brontë, March 2022

I am not a bird, and no net ensnares me.
               —Jane Eyre

To be unearthed at the International Antiquarian Book Fair—
no larger than a playing card, survived inside
some 19th-century schoolbook.

Who will vie for the priceless—
poor brown paper stitched with coarse thread, words
crossed out and corrected, infinitesimal
scratchings of a girl-woman announcing:

Attempts at rhyming of an inferior nature, Jane
not yet stirring, not yet tapping
from inside the egg
into an astounded world.

When Any Word Came Near Emily Dickinson's Name

after a line from William Stafford

Would it gasp or blush,
bow in deference: *I am at your call.*

would it pulse and glow

arriving at first breath,

trembling, like Bernadette
standing in the grotto   gazing up

Some Advice from Emily

Keep words
brief, bound-tight

think of that quick-startle—
fingertip on stovetop—

that one breath, throat-caught
seconds before the reveal.

Applied Literature

Too late for a hotel, an acquaintance offers us
this house high up in the village,
abandoned but for her brother's mattress
and chairs, the dust and grit of the Greek
island year sealing every surface, no heat
and the Cycladic wind like a creature rising lashing
and slapping the stone walls where we tried hard
to sleep, wind moaning (I finally decided)
like a grieving and venemous Heathcliff, beloved
book of my girlhood, and I with the chance to become
Catherine Earnshaw for one night as I pulled open
the split wood door into the howling darkness; my long, pale
nightgown billowing around my bare legs as I stumbled
outside—my moor—toward the one working place to pee.

Emily Dickinson on Apple TV

I love her belted plaid dresses
(years before the White commandment).
I love her auburn hair tousled and swaying
as she kisses her secret love Sue,
walks alongside the sexy editor Samuel Bowles.

Contrary to everything—this Emily
wants her poem on the front page
of the *Springfield Republican!*
She wants fame,
she fears fame
that turns her Invisible for a day.

Really, she is most at home
skipping another party,
hopping a quick ride on Death's carriage
as it passes by the Homestead yet again,
its silvery ghost horses stepping proud (high)
along the dusty Amherst roads.

At the Gym with the Brontës

Briskly walking and never arriving,
I feel slightly silly,
my gaze bobbing under florescent light
as I try to read the pages of *Jane Eyre*
weighted down on the metal tray.
Behind it, flashing red tells me
if my heart is doing its work,
if I've lopped off the damage
from last night's pie,

though I'm certain Emily and Charlotte,
even Anne, never thought of calories as
they trod their restless moors.
What on earth would they say about
exercising a body where
there is no soul to expand it,
no hems grazed by dirt and gorse,
nor hairs wrestled and undone
by a zealous wind while curlews swoop
and shriek in assent.

At the Mall Cineplex

Herded into the narrow aisles,
I can't help thinking of the Fox Bay Theater
on long Saturday afternoons;
the high school kids in burgundy blazers
ushering us into the hushed generous darkness
smelling of spilled popcorn
and thrumming with the promise
of a double feature, permission
to empty our boxes of Milk Duds
and JuJu Bees, our Charleston Chews
and tall cups of Hi-C,
the dark velvet drapery rolling open,
maneuvered by careful, invisible hands
while far away on the walls—the relief sculptures
of gnarled, windswept trees,
cliffs where a heroine might perch
awaiting her story.

Two Emilys

Who can say what happens
to a woman alone in her room,
with sheer white drapes trembling in air
rushing invisibly over her letters to the world,

or, when she leaves the walls behind her,
deskbox propped under arm,
mastiff sniffing the ground at her side,
the fierce countenance of the crags,
the wind's holler making translations in her body.

On the Day of the Book Launch

The velvet folds of her dress drape
on their hanger.
The lint roller is ready for duty.

She checks in the mirror for
a glint in her eyes,
an unclenching in her hands.

She knocks on the poem doors:
Are you ready?

About the Author

Andrea Potos is the author of seven full-length poetry collections, most recently *Her Joy Becomes* (Fernwood Press) and *Marrow of Summer* (Kelsay Books). A new collection from Fernwood Press entitled *Belonging Songs* will be published in 2025.

She is the recipient of five Outstanding Achievement Awards in Poetry from the Wisconsin Library Association and the James Hearst Poetry Prize from the *North American Review.*

Andrea's poems are published online and in print, including in *The Sun, One Art, Midwest Quarterly, Paterson Literary Review, Poem, Poetry East, Braided Way, Potomac Review,* and three anthologies from Storey Publishing, including *How to Love the World: Poems of Gratitude and Hope.*

She lives in Madison, Wisconsin.

www.ingramcontent.com/pod-product-compliance
Lightning Source LLC
Chambersburg PA
CBHW030815090426

42737CB00010B/1282